The 4 Keys

to Doubling your Business

David Holland MBA

© Copyright 2012 David Holland

978-1-291-22706-2

All rights reserved

Contents

INTRODUCTION 5

#1 - EXTERNAL MARKETING & SALES...............9

#2 – CUSTOMER SERVICE 15

#3 – INTERNAL SALES & MARKETING 24

#4 – EFFICIENCY AND PRODUCTIVITY 31

Gross Margin 36

Overheads. 38

THE SEVEN SACRED ELEMENTS 40

The Seven Elements Table..44

ABOUT RESULTS RULES OK 50

The 4 Keys

to Doubling your Business

Introduction

When I first entered the world of Coaching, Personal Development and Business Growth I quickly learned that there are plenty of labels applied to strategies and tactics that everyone uses naturally – but because there is a label applied to them they have to be relearned and we all have to be Master Wizard Practitioners of some latest craze in order to be able to achieve anything in life.

I remember going to a Workshop during which I was told that I had self-limiting beliefs, needed to get a "towards vision" for myself and that reciting positive incantations whilst tapping my head would be my "cure".

I wondered how I had managed to achieve anything in my life without tapping my head; it turns out that the "Master Wizard" taking the course had travelled less, achieved less and earned significantly less than most people in the room – and yet he was suggesting that we were broken and that he could fix us.

As with so many people in this sector they come into it for a variety of reasons;

1. **They want to help people** – great go work with a Charity.
2. **The need help / therapy themselves** – good, go and get it.
3. **They are unemployable** – so they aren't able to do anything else.
4. **They have read a book** – and think that everyone should live by it.

I should add that there are some great people in this sector, those who truly add value to people's lives with their ideas, strategies and tactics that enable people to become more successful – they have usually achieved something before they became Coaches and not simply as a consequence of it however – these are the people that are inspiring and motivational, who educate and train from a position of knowledge and experience – not hope and deluded self-belief.

There – *I feel better now…*

Sometime ago I was introduced to the work of W Edwards Deming – who in 1948 arguably created a system for Quality Management that would later become known as TQM. Taking his ideas to Japan after they were rejected by the USA Motor Manufacturers, he became instrumental in the development of Japanese Manufacturing methodologies.

He achieved amazing things in his life – I'm pretty sure he didn't need incantations or head tapping either – and his teachings are an inspiration to managers and entrepreneurs all over the world.

His books are available and to find out more information, simply search online for him and you will find plenty of data. At the risk of reducing his work to a simple list, the following is W. Edwards Deming's 14 Point Plan for transforming Business Effectiveness; taken from his book Out of The Crisis.

1. Create constancy of purpose toward improvement of product and service.
2. Adopt the new philosophy.
3. Cease dependence on inspection to achieve quality. Eliminate the need for massive inspection by building quality into the product in the first place.
4. End the practice of awarding business on the basis of a price tag. Instead, minimize total cost.
5. Improve constantly and forever the system of production and service, to improve quality and productivity, and thus constantly decrease costs.
6. Institute training on the job.
7. Institute leadership.
8. Drive out fear, so that everyone may work effectively for the company.
9. Break down barriers between departments.

10. Eliminate slogans, exhortations, and targets for the work force asking for zero defects and new levels of productivity.
11. Eliminate work standards on the factory floor. Substitute with leadership. Eliminate management by objective.
12. Remove barriers that rob the hourly worker of his right to pride of workmanship.
13. Institute a vigorous program of education and self-improvement.
14. Put everybody in the company to work to accomplish the transformation.

Essentially, what I believe he is saying is, focus on the causes of excellence. Focus on the factors that contribute to the desired result, rather than the result itself – simply looking at the Objective will not deliver excellence.

And – you really don't need to tap your head while doing incantations…

So this book aspires to use the philosophy of W. Edwards Deming, and describe a system that can be used to manage the contributory factors that deliver results in business, and enable a structured, predictable and repeatable way – success is the result of the disciplined application of a system of excellence – it is not the result of simply thinking positive thoughts and hoping for the best…

The spread sheet tools that are described in this book are available FREE from our website on the Resources Page – http://www.resultsrulesok.com/sign-up.php

#1 - External Marketing & Sales

 There are two main aspects of External Sales and Marketing, and each requires different measures applied.

External Marketing.

Everything that we do in business is Marketing – how we dress, our website, business cards, reputation, social media and even simply how we treat other people.

The purpose of Marketing is simply to get the 'phone to ring – could be a metaphorical 'phone of course, and could be in the form of a click on a website, response to an email or agreement to a meeting.

Remember in the SME sector we are not in the business of building brands, we are building a network and a reputation – we have to sell to people who have never heard of us, so our approach needs to be tailored accordingly.

The recognised "catch all" phrase associated with this activity is Lead Generation – and the measure of any marketing strategy is its ability to generate these responses.

External Sales.

Literally this is the ability of the organisation, the people within it or the technology it surrounds itself with to convert an enquiry, prospect, lead, call or meeting into an order.

The conversion of what I will collectively call "leads" will define the ability of the business to attract new clients.

Measuring the effectiveness of any Sales Strategy is simply its ability to convert Leads to Orders – measuring the Conversion Rate, usually as a Percentage is a simple and easy Key Performance Indicator.

As a tip – most people assume that their conversion rate is higher than it actually is. I worked with a client who thought that his conversion rate was 75%. We measured it and it was actually just 39% - he was horrified. However, this is a great opportunity in reality – we can't double 75%, but we can double 39%...

Once we understand the differences between the two, we can choose strategies for implementation and measure the results – if we can't measure it we can't manage it.

Key Performance Indicators.

Overall we will need to measure the effectiveness of both Marketing and Sales – but the combination of the two will determine our Acquisition Cost – what does it actually cost us to attract a new customer to our business..?

Marketing – here are some examples for measuring effectiveness.

Leads Generated per;

- 100 Telephone calls.
- 100 Letters or Direct Mail.
- 1000 Emails.
- LinkedIn Promotion
- Ad Word activity
- SEO strategy
- Networking Event.

The list is not exhaustive – but goes to show, that whatever activity we undertake, we need to measure the results.

For example; using Telesales to demonstrate the principle.

We can expect that a Telemarketer will make around 100 handset movements each day, out of those 100 these could be the results;

60 – Person not available or left the company.
20 – Not interested.
12 - Interested but not now – call back later.
5 - Interested – send information.
3 – Appointment booked

We also know that on average for every 3 appointments booked, one will cancel or postpone – so the real outcome of the day's activity is – Two Appointments.

Now, let's say that you pay your Telemarketer £15.00 per hour and he works for 8 hours per day – a day rate of £120.00

Cost of each appointment is
£120.00 / 2 = £60.00 each.

If you are selling a product with a Gross Margin of £50.00 – you have lost already. Your marketing must be proportionate to your product or service.

Now it is over to the Sales Team to convert the Prospect into a Customer.

Sales – measuring effectiveness.

Using the same example, let's assume that the Marketing Team have passed the details of the booked appointments to the Sales Team – for this example we will assume that someone has to meet with the prospect face to face and close the deal.

Let's say that we have two sales people, each being given leads by the Marketing Team, and here is what happens;

The first Sales person – Chris, has ten appointments booked in a week. He attends every meeting and at the end of the week has "converted" 4 new customers.

Chris has a conversion rate of – (4 /10) x100%

In other words his conversion rate is 40%

The second Sales Person – Helen, also has 10 appointments booked in a week. She attends every one and at the end of the week has "converted" 8 new customers.

Helen has a conversion rate of – (8 /10) x100%

In other words his conversion rate is 80%

So what – they are both bringing in Sales..?

What we are interested in here is the Acquisition Cost.

For Chris, the cost of bringing a new Customer into the business is

$$\frac{\text{\underline{Leads x Cost of Leads}}}{\text{New Customers}}$$

$$\frac{10 \times £60}{4} = £150$$

For Helen, the cost of bringing a new Customer into the business is;

$$\frac{\text{\underline{Leads x Cost of Leads}}}{\text{New Customers}}$$

$$\frac{10 \times £60}{8} = £75.00$$

So Helen is much more efficient at closing the deal when compared to Chris – it costs just £75.00 to get a customer when she closes the deal compared to £150.00 when Chris does it.

What this enables us to do is to look at what Helen is doing, and encourage Chris to do the same to improve his performance – if we don't measure their results, we can't manage their activities.

Now, if you knew that every time you spent £75.00 you would get a new customer, how many times would you do it…?

Answer – as many times as you like, because now you have a prove method of attracting customers. It gives us predictability and confidence that when we invest in marketing and selling, we are actually getting a return.

Clearly the actual statistics will be different from business to business, but the principle stays the same. In terms of continuous improvement, once we know our numbers we can constantly seek to improve them.

Rather than simply giving the Marketing Team or Sales Team a Budget to achieve – they can have a number of Key Performance Contributors – KPC's. If we manage our cost of generating appointments, and the conversion rate we achieve from them – the actual sales figure will look after itself.

We are looking at the factors that contribute to the outcome, not the outcome itself, understanding, measuring and improving our KPC's is the basis for these first two of what we will call the Seven Sacred Elements of Business Success; Prospects and Conversion Rate – Mr Deming would be proud of us.

#2 – Customer Service

 Customer Service is something that should be built in to your company. It starts with the Vision and Mission and is defined by the Culture and the People you employ.

It doesn't matter what business you are in – you will have competitors. They may be either direct service or product competitors or simply expenditure competitors; those who are competing, not with you, but for the discretionary cash those customers may have.

I will use Accountants as an example…

If you were to line up 6 Accountants, ask them why you should select them to represent you, and then you were asked to select one to be your service provider; how would you choose…?

If there was no tangible difference between their services, perceived reliability, quality and personality – you would probably differentiate on Price and choose the one that was towards the bottom of the range.

Customer Service is one of the key opportunities we have to achieve competitive advantage through positive differentiation and also in my view, one of the most overlooked.

Remember, you are not in the Accounting, Construction, Web Design etc. business; you are in the Customer Service business and the levels of service you provide will dictate your pricing, customer loyalty and ability to achieve profitable growth.

There are a number of KPC's related to Customer Service that can be helpful.

In one of my other books – *Strength in Numbers* – I discuss the attributes of finding out what your Customers actually think about you by asking them "The Ultimate Question" and recording / managing the results.

The number of referrals and introductions that Customers make is another good tangible indicator of how you are doing, as is the number of testimonials you receive.

For our purposes, and the third of our Sacred Elements, we will use Retention as the test of how effective the levels of Customer Service actually are. Retention is the ability of a company to keep clients coming back every year (we will look at the pace of activity later).

If for example a business has 150 customers buying from it in one financial or calendar year and of those 150, just 100 continue to buy from it in the following year, the Retention Rate of that business is;

$$\frac{\text{Customers Year 2}}{\text{Customers Year 1}} \times 100\%$$

$$\frac{100}{150} \times 100\% = 67\%$$

There are a few rules surrounding Customer Service, including;

- **Service is dependent upon the perception of your customers** – as business owning entrepreneurs we have our own ideas about what Customer Service looks like. The challenge is that what we think is amazing may not be the same as our customers do.

There is a further complication here, the old saying that in order to give great service all we need to do is give customers what they want. What they want may not be what they pay for; and in reality they don't know what they want.

For evidence of this, take a look at the video titled "Spaghetti Sauce" delivered by Malcolm Gladwell on www.ted.com, an elegant explanation of why we have some many different types of sauce available – and how they were developed; lessons for all of us in business.

Giving a Customer experience that they perceive as fabulous means that we have to give them not what they want, but what they have yet to discover they want.

Now, there are a few basic rules that always work when it comes to service including being on time, courteous, keeping promises and delivering what was ordered. These are the basics and everyone expects these to be in place as a matter of course.

It is the higher levels of service that define excellence – what else is being done to give your customers an experience they will remember, talk about and remind them of where they need to come back to next time.

The best way I have found to understand the perceptions of my customers is to only attract those people that appreciate what we do, like my style and approach and who don't take themselves too seriously. The trick is to only work with people that appreciate your style – and this comes down to targeting when it comes to Marketing and Lead Generation.

What is the best way to get a great conversion rate…?

Only go and see people who want to buy from you…

What is the best way of getting people raving about what you do…?

Work with people who like your style and appreciate what you do…

- **It has to be profitable to you** – there is a well-known story that tells how an employee of FedEx chartered an Executive Jet to deliver a single parcel for a customer, because the normal routes of distribution would not have enabled the delivery to be made.

  Now, whilst this is great PR and it is a great way of demonstrating commitment to get the job done – in the SME sector if we start doing this kind of thing on a regular basis, we will be out of business.

  Great Customer Service is not spelled "Discount" – it is for us to find ways of delivering a great product, service and experience that still means we can make a profit. In fact the whole intention of being so good is that we make more profit not less…

  The first rule of Sales and Customer Service is that customers don't buy on price – unless you let them, or encourage them.

I remember buying my first car in the USA – it was from Integrity Chrysler, Jeep and Dodge in Las Vegas, just after we moved there. I wanted a full size SUV, V8 with all the trimmings, seemed like a good idea at the time…

In the showroom was a Ford Expedition 5.4 V8 – Eddie Bauer – in other words a top of the range vehicle in the right colour and at the right price – $24,000. I was buying with £ Sterling at a rate of what was 2:1 – this was a cheap car for me.

I looked over the car, took it for a test drive and was really pleased; it had just about everything I wanted. I agreed to go into the dealership to raise the necessary paperwork – as the Salesman escorted me to the showroom he said "of course we don't expect you to pay full ticket price for that car, we can work a deal out.."

Up until that point, I had not intended to drive a deal. I would have had a go, and maybe gone for a tank of gas and some new floor mats, but as he said this a whole new world of possibilities opened up – he gave me permission to haggle on the price.

After about 20 minutes of "discussion" I ended up offering him my credit card saying – "take $15,000 off that I will take the car of your hands..."

He came back and said that he couldn't do that low and that the best he could do was $15,200 – I shook hands and bought my truck.

It has been a magnificent vehicle. We drove it all over California, Arizona, Texas and Nevada we have been to Death Valley, Lake Havasu, Las Vegas and

San Francisco – it has even been driven through a Giant Redwood.

We exported it to France when we moved to Europe and it has taken us to Belgium, Germany, Luxembourg, Monaco, Italy, Spain amongst others – it has never missed a beat and is still a great car to own – I would have paid full price for this car, and yet I was given permission to haggle.

Are you or your team giving your customers permission to haggle, or an excuse to spend more money and stay with you for years..?

Integrity Chrysler, Jeep and Dodge went in to liquidation citing the economy. They never thought to look at their levels of service and ambition to not make a profit.

- **Service has to be delivered consistently;** even predictable mediocrity will beat occasional excellence. One of the most valuable attributes of Customer Service is predictability. Customers want to know what to expect – yes it's great to impress them with something amazing from time to time, but the base level of service must be consistently and predictably high.

The levels of service in French restaurants are consistent and predictable – the problem is that they are consistently awful, and the same applies to most retail stores, banks or public services. It is as if customers somehow disturb their day, disrupt what would otherwise be a relaxing opportunity for them to chat with their workmates.

In Metz, where we live, there is a small restaurant called La Cloche. It sits opposite the large cathedral and only seats around 20 people. Sometime ago we went there on a Saturday evening; something was different…

All the staff were friendly, attentive and engaging; they even compensated for our French not being perfectly fluent. At 21.30 they asked if we would like to stay and join in the party with the other customers, we chatted to French, Germans, Austrians and Italians – everyone was friendly and it was a great evening.

Too good to be true we thought…

A few weeks later we decided to go again – and it was the same, which was really unusual, especially in France. We have been several times, and every time the food is excellent, the staff are warm and inviting and we have a great time. So much so that I write about them in my books, tell the story at workshops, and take friends and clients there on a regular basis.

Customer Service shines through all that you do – if we are honest, we know that the standards of service generally are rubbish – this gives us a great opportunity to look at what we do, make it consistently fabulous and develop our reputation accordingly.

- **It cannot be dependent on you** – it has to be delivered by your team, even when you are not there. Systems are the key – once you have a great business, the only way to grow and develop it without your direct involvement, is through systemising and continuous training. Training is a process not an event...

The Franchise industry has made this into an art form – whether you like it or not McDonalds have built a great business serving an average product. Their success is their attention to detail and systemising the experience so that it is always the same – they get 17 year old kids to run a global business that delivers 17% net profit.

Do McDonalds sell you a quality Burger..?

Yes – because a McDonalds burger that conforms to the specification of a McDonalds is the best quality it can be. It may not be the highest standard burger in the world, but they brilliantly deliver consistent, predictable quality and that is what makes them so special.

The owner of a McDonalds doesn't have to go there very often, they don't serve behind the counter and the levels of service and quality are dependent upon the systems, training and discipline applied – and not dependent upon whether the owner is there or not.

In my book Your Business Rules OK, I suggest that approaching your business as if it was a franchise is the best way to achieve consistent success – it doesn't means you should actually franchise, just that the principles are solid. I also give you the Eight Rules to follow that will guide you on how to achieve it.

- **The service that your company provides must be unique, and able to identify your company as different from others** – what we are looking for is differentiation, not simple duplication of what others are doing. La Cloche in Metz is truly unique, some people may like a more formal dining experience, but we love it. It may not appeal to everyone, but it appeals to enough people to make it a great business.

When defining your unique customer service experience, don't just copy the others in your field, innovate and create something unique and special, something that supports your Vision and engages not just your customers but your team too.

What happens when you are not there is the true test of Customer Service, and the people you recruit to work with you will define your standards and success in this area – coupled with continuous training and development of course.

#3 – Internal Sales & Marketing

Overlooked by the majority of Business Owners, this area of the business when implemented correctly will transform your results by maximising the return you get from all your customers.

There is an unfortunate belief that the only way to grow a business is through the attraction of new Customers – attracting new customers could be one of the last things you should do; maximising the ones that you already have could also be one of the first.

Some simple steps that you should take to make sure that you are maximising the benefit your business derives from your existing customers include making sure the other Keys are being fully implemented. This may sound a bit simple but it is true – the best way to get customers to spend more with you is to be consistently excellent for example. The Four Keys are intertwined – you really can't do them in isolation.

So what are the measures or KPC's for this aspect of your business – what does Mr Deming expect us to do here..?

The first measurement is the Fourth Sacred Elements and is known as the Average Order Value of each purchase made. There are a number of calculations that can be helpful here.

How to calculate the Average Order Value for your business.

This is a simple formula;

Total Annual Sales
Number of Invoices

So for example let's say we have a business with total sales of £2,818,000 and the number of Invoices raised in the year is 3,462 – then we can work out the value.

$\frac{£2,753,780}{2,840}$ = Average Order Value

£969.64 = Average Order Value

So for this business, the Average Order Value is £969.64, now we can put strategies in place to improve this – remember if it can't be measured it can't me managed.

Now, in most businesses, different customers may have different average values – you may find that some customers buy large amounts and some who buy smaller amounts. We can also look for other indices from the sales ledger to help us.

The Average Order Value per customer is calculated in the same way as the average for the whole business – just using individual customer results. These results can then be plotted on a graph for example so that a complete picture of the business can be seen.

Imagine the above company has measured not just the Average Order Value, but also looked at the spread of the individual order values too. The table below shows the Value of Orders and also the number of times they occur during the year.

This analysis can be done for individual customers too – to see what the spread of order values actually is, there is a danger when working with blunt averages, we usually need to go a couple of layers deeper to find out what is going on.

So, here is the raw data – what can we tell from this..?

We know that the Average Order Value is £969.64 – now we can see the spread.

Plotting these figures onto a simple chart means we can see what is really going on.

Occurrence	Order Value
150	100
250	200
350	300
400	400
250	500
150	600
100	700
0	800
10	900
20	1000
0	1100
0	1200
0	1300
10	1400
0	1500
0	1600
150	1700
250	1800
450	1900
300	2000
2840 Total Orders	£2,818,000 Total Sales

The Order Value is shown on the Horizontal Axis – x £100, and the Occurrences are plotted against the Vertical Axis.

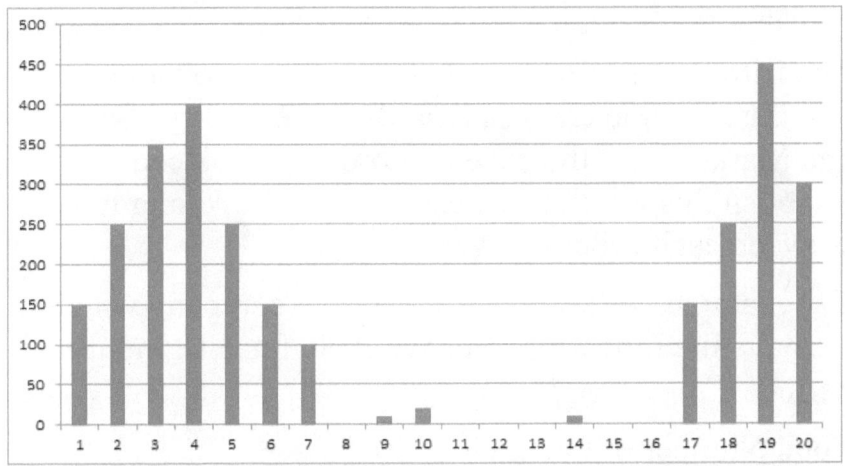

As we can see the Customer very rarely places Orders that are the same as the Average of £969.64, most of the Orders are either much larger or significantly smaller.

We can also tell that based on the data;

- The top 40% of Orders represent 77% of the Total Sales.
- The Bottom 50% of Orders represents just 16% of the Total Sales.

Questions we can ask ourselves now would include;

- Are we making any money on the smaller orders…?
- Where is the Margin being made, on the larger or smaller orders…?
- What is the Transaction Cost of each order as % of the Margin achieved…?
- Can we encourage the "bundling" of smaller orders for efficiency…?
- Do we need to offer all these services or products…?

The same analysis can be carried out with regards to Gross margin, and then ideal and minimum Order Values can be calculated – and our pricing strategy adjusted accordingly.

The fifth Sacred Element that contributes towards making strategic choices regarding the Internal Sales and Marketing is the pace that orders are placed. To establish this we simply need to know how long it is between each order on average.

For example, let's say that we have a company where we have the following data available for a 12 month period

Total Number of Orders = 2840

Total Number of Customers = 200

From this we can calculate the Average Number of Orders received from each Customer.

$$\frac{\textbf{Total Orders}}{\textbf{Total Customers}} = \textbf{Average \# Orders}$$

$$\frac{2840}{200} = \text{Average \# Orders}$$

$$14 = \text{Average \# Orders}$$

So the first step is clear – on Average, our Customers are placing Orders 14 times each year. This is an interesting statistic in itself; however, we are looking for a method of not only measuring but managing the business, so we need to look deeper.

What we are really interested in is how long is the interval between orders – such that if know what the expected "delay" is we can set up systems that flag up to our teams when an Order can be expected, and if one is not received, we can contact the Customer and find out why the pattern has changed – a great way of managing your Customer base.

To calculate how long on Average it is between Orders;

$$\frac{52 \text{ Wks}}{\text{Ave \# Orders}} = \text{Ave Wks between Orders}$$

$$\frac{52 \text{ Wks}}{14} = \text{Ave Wks between Orders}$$

$$\frac{52 \text{ Wks}}{14} = 3.7 \text{ Wks between Orders}$$

So in this business we know that on Average we get an Order from each Customer every 3.7 weeks – for Operational requirements, let's call it every 4 weeks.

As we found with the Average Order Value, there are a number of variables that may be required to be taken into consideration when it comes to the analysis of the date and the strategic choices made – the emphasis is simple, however, how do we reduce the time in between Orders?

Issues to watch out for include;

- **Seasonal businesses;** where the pattern of Orders may change during the year.

- **Timing;** of Big Orders as Opposed to Smaller Ones.

- **Call Off;** when a bulk order is placed and delivery is on a call off basis.

- **Sales Ledger;** the difference between Orders received and Invoices Raised.

Another, KPC that Mr Deming would approve of…

#4 – Efficiency and Productivity

Not the sexy end of the Business – always amazes me that the world is full of Sales and Marketing Master Wizards, but most of them tend to avoid the basics of business,; the basics that are fundamental to your success, and can help you make more money by actually doing less.

I trained as a Production Engineer, involved in the batch manufacturing of assault rifles, machine guns and cannon. My job was relatively straight forwards; I had to balance three aspects of the production process.

a. **Quality** – maintaining the quality of the components produced such that the assembled weapons were fit for purpose. Quality was measured by gauges and specialist measuring devices to ensure that the manufacturing tolerances, finishes and properties were achieved to an acceptable level; the amount of scrap or rework was kept within target ranges.

b. **Efficiency** – the attendance and application of the machines and people under my control. Efficiency is a measure of the application of resources compared with their total availability.

For example;

Imagine a worker is employed for 8 hours per day, 5 days per week. Over a 52 week year the worker is available for work for 52 x 40hrs = 2080 hrs.

This is the maximum that a person can work without overtime. However, it is unlikely that the worker will be engaged in work continuously for each of the 2080 hours – here's what can change the value.

I. Holidays –28 Days @ 8 hrs. per day = 224 hrs.
II. Sickness –10 Days @ 8Hrs. per day = 80 hrs.
III. Waiting time –annual value = 200 hrs.
IV. Wandering about –annual value = 200 hrs.
V. Rest Breaks –annual value = 150 hrs.
VI. Chatting –annual value = 200 hrs.
VII. Procrastination –annual value = 200 hrs.
VIII. Mistakes / Rework –annual value = 200 hrs.

Now these figures are made up – but in reality, they are not that far away from actual results in some organisations.

So given the data above, we can work out the actual number of hours that can be applied to productive work as a percentage of the total available – a measure of productivity.

Efficiency % = Productive Hrs. / 100
             Available Hrs.

Efficiency % = (576 Hrs. / 2080 Hrs.) /100

Efficiency = 28%

So based on the data – this business or department on average is just 28% efficient – in other words, 72% of the available time is being allocated to activities other than productive work.

Productivity – the rate of output achieved for every unit of resource utilised.

For example, one of my production lines was involved with the manufacture of firing pins for assault rifles – and I would measure the productivity on the basis of output per hour.

If during a year, using the data above a team of 10 staff produced 250,000 firing pins – this is how we would calculate the Productivity of the line.

Productivity = # Parts / Productive Hrs.

Productivity = 250,000 / (576 hrs. x 10)

Productivity = 250,000 / 5760 hrs.

Productivity = 43 components per hour

This equates to a total of 1.38 minutes to produce each firing pin.

My challenge as a Production Engineer was to improve these results and therefore produce the Firing Pins to the required quality standards whilst improving both productivity and efficiency.

Now, if I asked the workers if they could achieve more – they would probably say that they didn't have time to make any more pins – they were busy already.

When we look at "time management" – which we now know is impossible; we tend to focus on how busy we are, not on how Productive or Efficient we actually are.

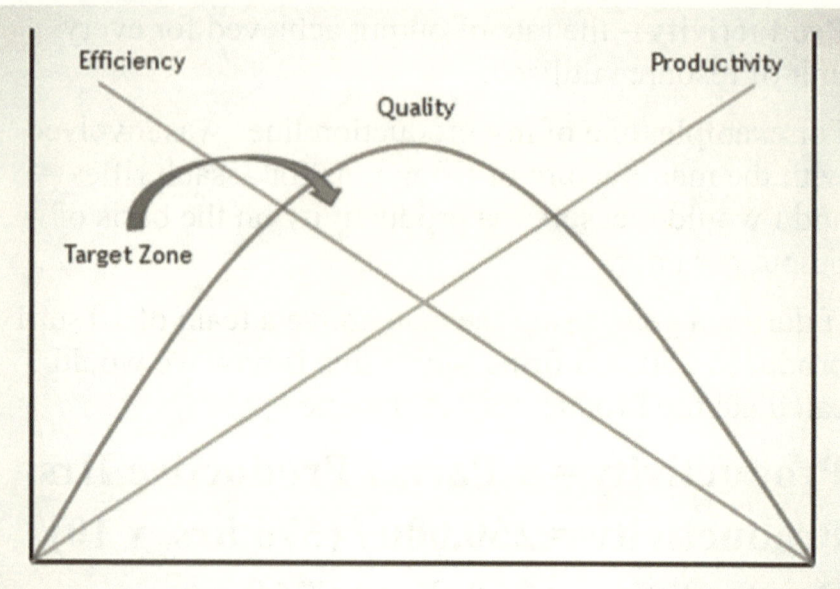

There is a clear relationship between the three aspects of Production – there is a fourth aspect that involves the degree of risk and danger to employees too – for now I am assuming that all Health and Safety regulations are being fully complied with. Again this may or may not be the case in some organisations.

The chart shows the relationship between the levels of Efficiency, Productivity and Quality expressed as a graph. Without going into all the intricate details there are a couple of Rules of Production that are worth bearing in mind.

> I. As Efficiency Increases – Productivity may Decline after a certain point indicated by where the lines cross – workers may not work faster just because they are productive for more time, in fact they may tend to slow down if they feel that "chatting" and "wandering around" time has been taken away from them.

II. As Productivity Increases – Quality may Decline when the curve begins to fall – speed is the enemy of Quality, so as the focus shifts to increase output, so must the emphasis be increased on the process and systems involved such that quality is maintained at acceptable levels.

III. As Quality Increases – Productivity may Decline – the converse of pt. 2 above.

So the question we have to ask ourselves when it comes to achieving more, is not simply look to do more – but look at how our time is actually being invested.

What is your actual Efficiency – how much time is really spent in the "wandering around" category – how much of your team's time is spent here…?

What is your productivity – are you working at optimum levels, or is quality suffering and causing rework and delays.

These two areas alone will free up time to be invested in productive activities – and they are so simple to measure and improve. This is a great place to start.

Now we have the final two of the Seven Sacred Elements that we can use to build our remarkable business; Gross Margin and Overheads.

Gross Margin

Gross Margin is basically the Total Sales value minus the Direct Costs associated with the production of the goods or the delivery of the service. Usually the Direct Costs will include Materials and Labour directly used in support of the Sales.

For example, and I will keep this one really simple...

Let assume that a company sells £750,000 of services in a month.

This company is a courier company, delivering parcels on behalf of customers.

Costs that would likely be classified as Direct Costs in this business would include;

- Wages of the Drivers.
- Fuel for the Vehicles.
- Rental cost for the Vehicles.
- Tolls and Charges for road use.
- Mobile phone costs for the drivers.

So the total Direct Cost of achieving the Sales could be as follows;

- Wages of the Drivers - £250,000
- Fuel for the Vehicles - £200,000
- Rental cost for the Vehicles - £100,000
- Tolls and Charges for road use - £20,000
- Mobile phone costs for the drivers - £5000

Total Direct Costs = £575,000

Gross Profit = Sales – Direct Costs

Gross Profit = £750,000 – £575,000

Gross Profit = £175,000

The Gross Profit can be expressed as a % of the Sales – it can also be known as Contribution (to fixed costs) too.

$$\text{Gross Margin \%} = \frac{\text{Gross Profit}}{\text{Total Sales}} \times 100$$

$$\text{Gross Margin \%} = \frac{£175,000}{£750,000} \times 100$$

Gross Margin = 23%

The key here is to understand the Gross Margin for your business, and then to put strategies in place to improve the % and the total value achieved.

Overheads.

The Overheads are all the costs associated with the running of a business that in the short term at least – are fixed irrespective of the levels of Sales or Production

Typically these include Rent, Rates, Staff Salaries and other costs of administration including Marketing and Sales.

Following on from the example above, let's assume that the company has Monthly Overheads of £125,000 – this value will dictate the Net Profit and margin % of the Business.

In this case the Net profit will be;

Net Profit = Gross Profit - Overheads

Net Profit = £175,000 - £125,000

Net Profit = £50,000

The Net Margin, expressed as a % can also be calculated as follows;

$$\text{Net Margin \%} = \frac{\text{Net Profit}}{\text{Total Sales}} \times 100$$

$$\text{Net Margin \%} = \frac{£50,000}{£750,000} \times 100$$

Net Margin % = 6.6%

Now, this is not intended to be an Accounting book – just an overview of some of the principles that can be helpful.

The emphasis is not to just reduce the Overheads but improve the efficiency of every £1 we spend – for example, in a growing business – do we need to increase the Overheads to cope with demand...?

Probably not in the short term, in the medium and long term we may need to take on bigger premises, hire more staff etc. These are known as "step costs" and can be predicted once we have control of the numbers.

Other additional measures that are interesting to keep under control rather than just the Gross and Net Margin include;

- **Overheads as a % of Total Sales**
- **Net Profit as a % of Overheads.**
- **Individual lines of Overheads as % of Sales.**
- **Productivity and Efficiency of Staff.**

The Seven Sacred Elements

In 1863, there were just 56 Elements known to man, although new ones were being discovered at the rate of around one per year.

On the 6th March 1869, Dmitri Mendeleev the Russian Chemist and Inventor, made a presentation to the Russian Chemical Society - The Dependence between the Properties of the Atomic Weights of the Elements.

He produced a Table that became known as the Periodic Table that arranges all the Elements according to their Atomic Weight and Valence.

All the Elements are distinct and have their own properties – remember in Chemistry when the teacher put some Sodium (Na) in water for example…

There are several Elements of running a business too, probably more than the number included in the current periodic table.

As with the Periodic Table – there are some Elements that are more significant than others, and these I have called the Sacred Elements…

1	2											13	14	15	16	17	18
H																	He
Li	Be											B	C	N	O	F	Ne
Na	Mg	3	4	5	6	7	8	9	10	11	12	Al	Si	P	S	Cl	Av
K	Ca	Sc	Ti	V	Cr	Mn	Fe	Co	Ni	Cu	Zn	Ga	Ge	As	Se	Br	Kr
R	Sr	Y	Zr	Nb	Mo	Tc	Ru	Rh	Pr	Ag	Cd	In	Sn	Sb	Te	I	Xe
Cs	Ba		Hf	Ta	W	Re	Oh	Ir	Pt	Au	Hg	Tl	Pb	Bi	Po	Aw	Rn
Fr	Ra		Rf	Db	Sg	Bh	Hs	Mt	Ds	Rg							

La	Ce	Pr	Nd	Pm	Sm	Eu	Gd	Tb	Dy	Ho	Er	Tm	Yb	Lu
Ac	Th	Pa	U	Np	Pu	Am	Gm	Bk	Cf	Es	Fm	Md	No	Lr

For our Purposes, and following on from the previous chapters, the Seven Sacred Elements of building your remarkable business are;

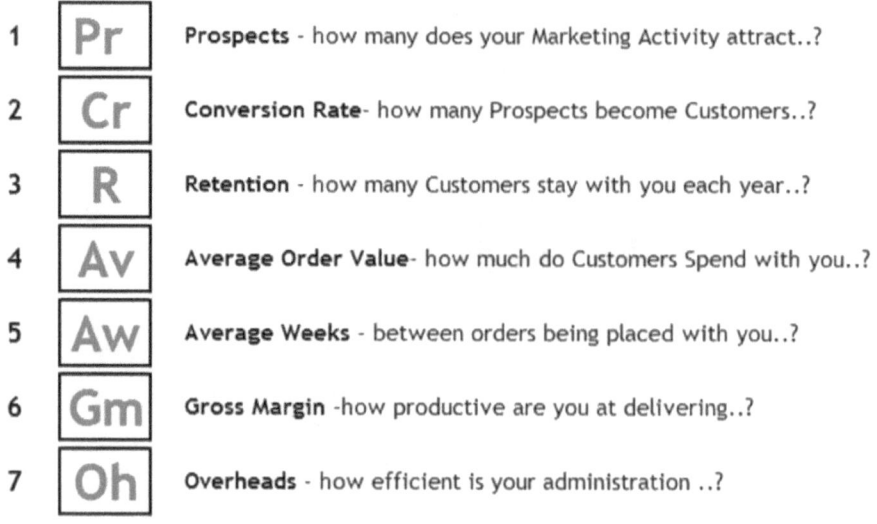

On the following tables, you will see how the Seven Sacred Elements can be used to improve any business – the Toolkit is available as **FREE** Download from our Website, go to http://www.resultsrulesok.com/sign-up.php

The Toolkit may suggest the Elements need to be used in sequence starting from top to bottom – they do not, in fact it is very likely that the last one you should consider is Prospects – we need to get everything else in the business running at maximum effectiveness before we start to bring in lots of new Customers.

The sequence is really dependent upon the business and the unique challenges and opportunities that you may face within your sector.

As a rule I would look at Overheads and Gross Margin first, and then Average Order Value and Average Weeks, followed by Retention and then Conversion Rate and Prospects – but the sequence is not fixed. For example, if we can get a quick win by improving the Conversion rate in your business within a few weeks – then that is a great start. We need to make sure that the other Elements are managed and improved as well but in reality we will take the benefits where we find them.

The Seven Elements Table

The Four Keys and the Seven Sacred Elements can be visually represented, and are shown on the table below – all the following tables have been taken from the Toolkit that you can download from our website.

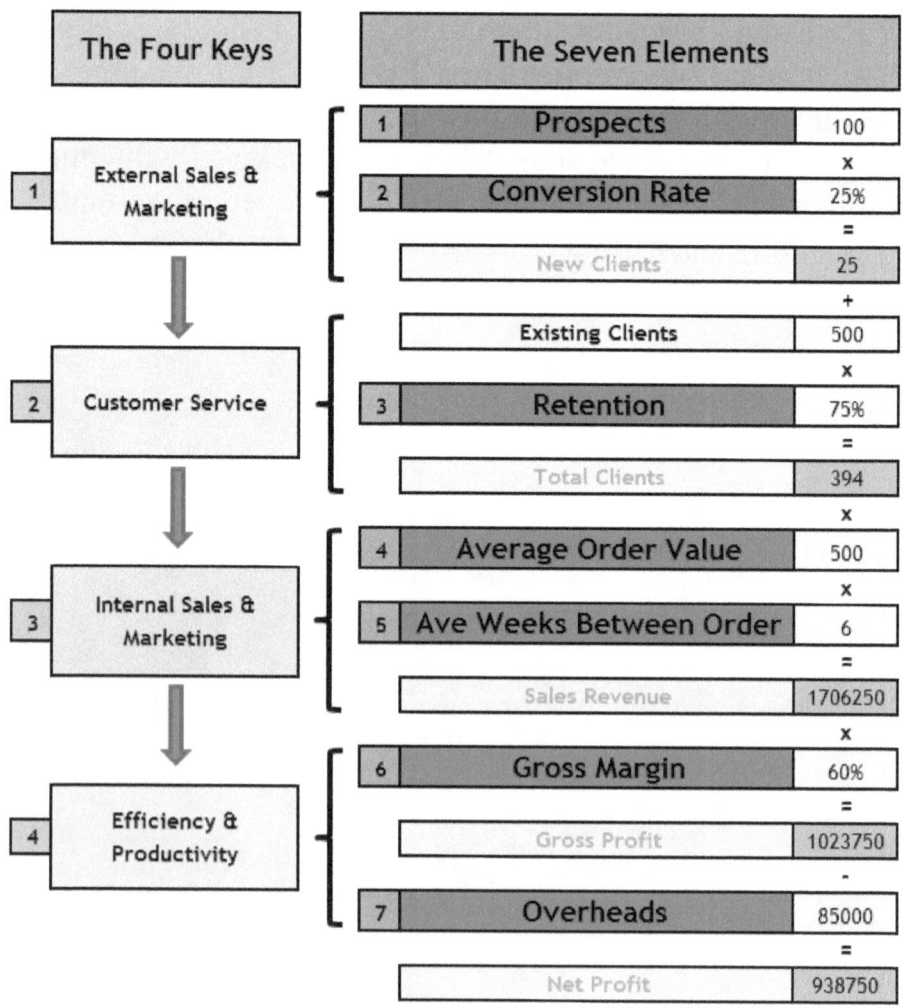

I have added some figures to each of the boxes to demonstrate how the process works. As you can see the Seven Sacred Elements combine to describe a business in terms of Clients, Sales Revenue, Gross Profit and Net Profit – these are our outcomes.

What we need to focus on is the factors that affect the outcomes – the causes not the symptoms.

The expanded Table shows how, from a planning perspective we can "play" or in correct terms "model" our business by adjusting each of the Seven Sacred Elements and seeing what the effect would be on the outcomes.

It may be of course that only some of the Elements will be adjusted upwards, it may be in fact that strategically, we actually reduce the value of some of the Elements; it will depend on your business and your personal Goals and Ambitions. Full instructions are included on the Toolkit.

The first job of course is to measure the performance of your Business in relation to the Seven Elements, and then you can make choices and adjustments to them to see what the effect would be.

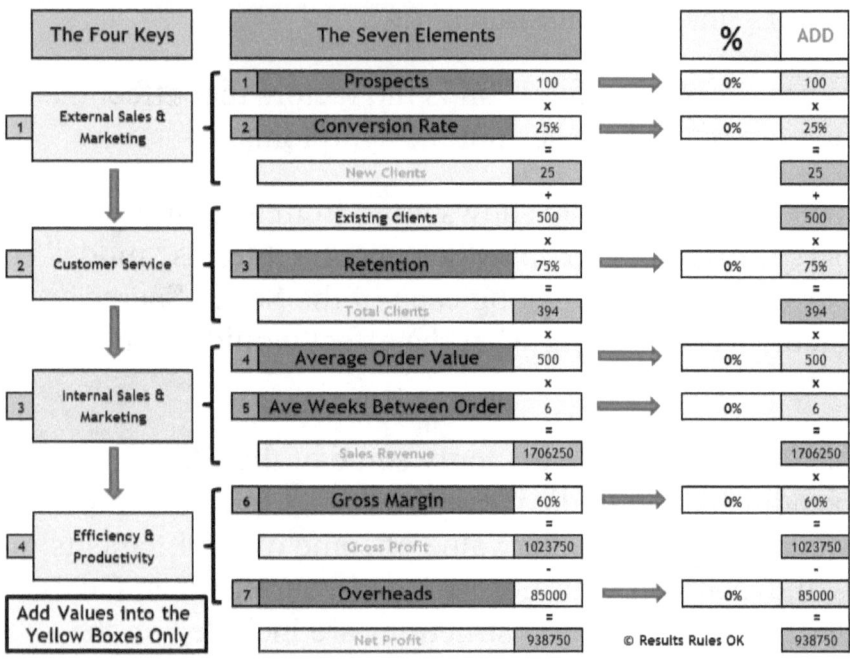

In order to help with the choices, there is a table of Strategies included in the Toolkit that may help you. As you make choices and make an assumption regarding the benefit to each of the Elements – the Table will automatically calculate the effects of your choices on the results of the business.

The Four Keys → The Seven Elements → Results RULES OK

Here are the top Strategies that can be used to improve each of the Seven Elements and deliver outstanding Results

© Results Rules OK

	Key # 1 External Sales & Marketing		Key # 2 Customer Service	Key # 3 Internal Sales & Marketing			Key # 4 Efficiency & Productivity	
	Prospects Lead Generation	Conversion Rate %	Retention %	Average Order Value	Average Weeks Between Order		Gross Margin %	Overheads Annual Total
1	LinkedIn	Sales Training	Client Survey - NPS	Up Sell	Closed Door Sale		Buy Better	Cut Costs
2	FaceBook	USP	Wow factor	Cross Sell	Maintenance Program		Reduce Wastage	Maximise Productivity
3	Networking	Why, What and Wow	Build Community	Bundling	Book next Visit		Maximise Productivity	Maximise Efficiency
4	Referrals	Guarantee	Relationship	Added Value	Extend Range		Maximise Efficiency	Subcontract
5	Alliances	Special Offers	News Letter	New Products	Service Visits		Reduce Theft	Use Freelancers
6	Joint Ventures	Sales System	LinkedIn	New Services	Themed Events		Re Design Product	Buy Premises
7	Video Uploads	Testimonials	FaceBook	Pricing	Buy Products In		Sub Contract	Staff Incentive Scheme
8	Book Writing	Samples	Staff Training	Special Offers	New Products		Own Brand Items	Rent out Space
9	Blog Posting	ABC - Always Be Closing	Vision	Closed Door Sale	New Services		Offer Finance	Move Location
10	Seminars	Bundling	Mission	No Discounts	Seasonal Offers		Negotiate Better	Go Paperless
11	Conference Speaking	Time limited Offers	Rules of the Game	Make Easy to Buy	Run a Competition		Do GAP Analysis	Use Skype for Calls
12	Workshops	Charity / Causes	Agreements	Bulk Offers	Loyalty Card		Refurbish Products	Audit Accounts
13	Radio Adverts	Payment Terms	Leadership	Enable Impulse Buys	Delivery Service		Team Incentives	Review all Costs
14	Website & SEO	Ease of Purchase	Keep in Touch	Publicise Entire Range	Kan Ban System		Vertical Integration	Check all Direct Debits
15	Direct Mail	Improve Packaging	Buy from Clients	Team Training	Hold Stock		Buy Competitors	Check Standing Orders
16	Email	Set Targets	Give Referrals	Horizontal Integration	Help Client Grow		Offer Additional Services	Invest Spare Cash
17	Telemarketing	BOGOF	Give Testimonials	Improve Quality			Reduce Reworking	Clear Overdraft
18	News Paper Adverts	Trial Periods		Limited time Offers				Clear Loans
19	On Line Directories	Offer Trade In						Clear all Credit Cards
20	Advertorials	Follow Up						Change Bank
21	Bold Calling							Maintenance Program
22	Exhibitions							
23								
24								
25								

47

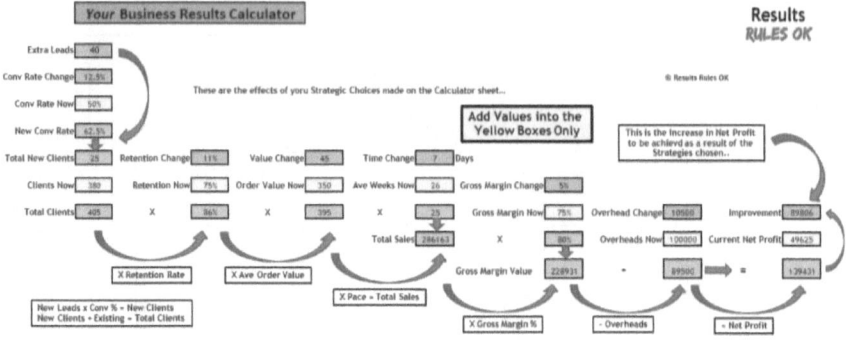

Another Table on the Toolkit will explain the consequences of your Choices and show how the calculation flows through the different areas.

This exercise is of course only productive if the ideas and strategies are actually implemented, so this should form your Business Planning activities – and become part of your 90 Day Planning exercise too.

Finally, please remember the concept of SMART when it comes to setting your Goals and objectives;

Specific

Measureable

Achievable

Realistic

Time Relative

For those that have ben to my workshops you will know that I change the A to Amazing and the R to Rewarding – who is to tell you what is Achievable and Realistic..?

Can you imagine when the Khufu planned the building of the Great Pyramid in Giza – it was not Realistic, and may have seemed Unachievable, but it was built all the same – the opportunity is to find a way…

So, I hope this Book has given some ideas, a method and a set of Tools that will help you build your remarkable business. Email me with any questions, or come along to one of our events and workshops – I look forward to hearing about your success…

About Results Rules OK

Results Rules OK was created with a simple and clear 2020 vision;

To enable everyone to enjoy learning, achieving, doing and being more...

This is achieved through the delivery of World Class Business Coaching, Training, and Development Programs designed for business owners and entrepreneurs just like you...

We recognise that all businesses are different, as are the people that build, own and run them so we have a range of products and programs that will help, inspire and support you – whatever stage of development your business is at...

You can register for our newsletter, check out David's latest blog and even download documents and templates from our website at www.resultsrulesok.com

If you'd like to come along to an event – either to join one of our Webinars or participate in a Workshop or Seminar – visit our website www.resultsrulesok.com to find our full schedule of events.

David is offers a limited number of FREE **Business Strategy Sessions** for qualifying businesses, to arrange a meeting or discussion with David, simply got to www.resultsrulesok.com, scroll down and press the **"Book Free Session with David"** button...

Our USP is our people, our delivery, the results our Clients achieve and our philosophy of Fun in Life and in Business. We are a growing profitable business, and we believe in making contributions to charity and causes that are aligned with our values.

David's unique experience, background and passion for adding value to the business and personal lives of others have enabled him to become not only a top Business Coach, but an accomplished Speaker and Author. Having worked in 21 countries so far, his presentations and key note presentations are compelling, informative and fun and his books reflect his knowledge and personality…

David's first two books are available now…

If you have got this far then maybe we should talk…!

Contact Us;

Web – www.resultsrulesok.com

Email – info@resultsrulesok.com

Other Books by David Holland now available

Business Results Rules OK Volume I

Business Results Rules OK Volume II

Life Results Rules OK Volume I

Only Read at 4am

Would you like Fries with That?

Is Business Coaching Hornswoggle

Learning How to Fly

Unlucky for Some

The Case of the Ego in the Corner

The YOU Tree

Lights, Camera, Action

Contrary to Popular Belief

Every Day in Every Way, I'm Getting Better & Better

Success Matters

Success Rules OK

Scared of the Dark?

Leads United

Selling & Closing

The Franchise Connection

The Professional Tarot

Goals, Objectives and Precession

How to Surf the Tsunami…

Strength in Numbers….

Dutch Courage...

Negotiating Success

The 9 Rules

Drumming and the Art of Business Maintenance

The 5 P's Professionals need to know

Growing Pains

Fractional Thinking

Customers for Life

Presenting Excellence

Goals Suck

Excellence is a Real Pitch

So Good they Rationed it

Getting Picked

Changing Rooms

Smoke, Mirrors and Overnight Success

The End is Nigh

Symbiotic Results

Back to Front Leadership

Seeing is Not Believing

The Silence of the Pigs

Questions from your Favourite Teenager

The Time that People Forgot

The How 2 Series

Results *RULES OK*
The *YOU* Tree

Business Coaching
FOR **Professionals**
BY **Professionals**

Looking for someone inspirational, competent but also kind & honest? He's THE guy. A true leader that's always there to make you better.'

"David Holland MBA is FUN, he is extremely engaging and shares his wisdom generously with an intent to always be of service to others."

'David is always able to add just the right bit of humour to his professional endeavours'

'David is a superb coach with extensive business experience and knowledge - oh, and one of the funniest people I have ever met! '

www.resultsrulesok.com

www.ingramcontent.com/pod-product-compliance
Lightning Source LLC
Chambersburg PA
CBHW021927170526
45157CB00005B/2213